blue
rider
press

THIS LAND WAS MADE FOR YOU AND ME
(BUT MOSTLY ME)

Also by Bruce McCall

50 Things to Do with a Book

Marvellown

All Meat Looks Like South America

The Last Dream-o-Rama

Thin Ice

Sit!: The Dog Portraits of Thierry Poncelet
(text by Bruce McCall)

Bruce McCall's Zany Afternoons

THIS LAND WAS MADE FOR YOU BUT MOSTLY ME AND ME

BILLIONAIRES IN THE WILD

Bruce McCall & David Letterman

BLUE RIDER PRESS
A member of Penguin Group (USA)
New York

THIS LAND WAS MADE FOR YOU AND ME
(BUT MOSTLY ME)

IT ALL BEGAN A DECADE AND A HALF AGO OR SO IN THE FAR American West, in Montana and Wyoming and those other states that appropriated and misspelled the Native American words for "Big Empty Space" and "Much Bigger Empty Space"; there, a few daring pioneers from the pharaonically wealthy top crust embarked on a spree, powered by a lust, inspired by a vision only they could see.

Because it takes more than money, privilege, and cronies in high places to ransack Nature's bounty for the private pleasure of the privileged few, in what the poets might call acts of sublime idiocy (as if anybody would ask *poets* their opinion!), in other words: obliterating what always was, and making out of it what never existed before, then flanking it with armed guards and electric fences and Rottweilers.

It takes a vision, indeed, that has swiftly metastasized into a contagion spreading through the Forbes 500 and across America and around the globe like an infestation of so many golden bedbugs nesting inside so many Fabergé eggs. A vision that sees molehills made into mountains and let the moles go hang. A vision of kaleidoscopic variety, yet harkening to the same swelling theme: *This land belongs to you and me, but mostly me.*

Celebrating this theme wherever it takes physical shape, by way of a simple formula of *outrageous fantasy* x *limitless money* x *ditto ego* x *that ineluctable thing some call megalomania,* wherever they combine and combust— and let's face it, that means everywhere and anywhere the elements are conquered, environmental common sense is flouted, and ecological dangers ignored—is one major mission of this book, second only to making money.

Fueled not only by insatiable greed but also by a near-religious zeal for innovation in the art and science of doing things with their fortunes that would thrombose Croesus himself, these swashbuckling billionaire trailblazers in pushing and ripping and otherwise savaging the envelope until it falls apart, as much as sneer, paraphrasing "Ozymandias": "Look upon my works, ye environmentalist sissies and ecology hysterics and tree-hugging, snail darter–addicted nerds, and try and stop us, because we have the politicians and the government and the regulators in our hip pocket. Not to even mention McCall and Letterman."

Who, for their part, have left word that they are traveling and unavailable for comment.

"GRAB THE POOCH, HERE COMES THE GULFSTREAM!"

A conventional outdoor landing strip would have been bad for the environment," explains Midas Upwith, heir to the Swill-Mart discount life fortune and master of the only Montana hunting lodge with its own indoor airport. "The planes landing and taking off would always be running over those armies of prairie dogs scooting across the tarmac, forcing us to bring in highly toxic chemicals to clean up the blood and guts," he adds.

"Plus, what the heck, we had plenty of room on the mezzanine floor after moving the working authentic Native American village and the den/rumpus room/library/gentleman's club down to the ground level."

Even after thousands of uneventful takeoffs and landings, Midas and the gang still drop what they're doing and watch with bated breath as another jet approaches, wings wagging this way and that until it slips through the arched Sky Door with only inches to spare, kisses the runway, and rolls to a stop in the living room.

And in—*mirabile dictu!*—almost perfect silence. "Sure, it cost a bundle to soundproof this place," Midas recalls. "But listen, when one of those jets roars in and the reverse thrusters kick in with that piercing shriek, you don't even have to turn up the volume on the TV. Truth to tell, however," he confides, "a little jet-engine whine is welcome around bedtime—just enough to drown out the yowling of that consarned pack of wolves the kids keep penned up in the rumpus room."

"He called it the Rhône Drone," recalls Runway Ranch owner Midas Upwith, speaking of the time the U.S. Poet Laureate ("His name will come to me in a minute," apologizes Midas) was a dinner guest and used his brilliant rhyming gifts to so dub the electronically guided miniature aircraft that ferries kegs of mein host's favorite Côtes du Rhône *vin rouge* on a twisting, turning fifteen-minute flight through the ranch's labyrinthine mezzanine level from the wine grotto to the dining hall. The drone, operated from the same control room that electronically oversees all indoor aviation in the ranch's main house, is often used as after-dinner entertainment— performing aerobatics and on special occasions smoking a giant cigar rolled from real Cuban tobacco leaves.

"A cigar-smoking airplane always draws lots of oohs and aahs," Midas affirms. "I don't know why it isn't more popular in other homes; all you need is a bellows in the nose of your drone and a guy back in the control room toggling a pulse switch so it puffs and draws and puffs and so on.

"Though I have to admit the ladies don't much go for it," he grins. "That Cuban tobacco is mucho strong stuff and smoking it in an enclosed space— even this one, which is bigger than the Pantheon in Rome—lays down a cloud of stink that could turn the stomach of a Cape buffalo."

"The picture's perfect-plus," exults Narco Jones, chatelaine of El Rancho Runway, "and you can turn dawn into dusk and vice versa just by turning a knob." Every balcony and sundeck in the place gives not onto majestic views of the surrounding natural scenery but a giant-screen HD-TV of the surrounding natural scenery. "We're on the perfectionist side," she burbles. "So when it comes to picture definition and fidelity, Nature runs a poor damn second to a good plasma HD television!" And, quoth she, the indoor show of the outdoors eliminates any reason for the Jones jaspers to stray outside—"where they could get snakebit, taken away by wolves, attacked by rabid prairie dogs, or kidnapped by terrorists," she shudders. "Or, worst-case scenario, get mud on those thousand-dollar alligator cowboy boots."

Practical concerns do sometimes intrude. Example: a runway-cum-floor made of painstakingly cut and fitted mahogany planks *can* make things tricky for unsuspecting pilots. Without a masterly touch on the controls, the plane can slip and slide on that slick waxed surface as the tires struggle to get a grip. "But the wife couldn't abide the idea of an asphalt strip running straight through the middle of the lodge," sighs Midas Upwith.

"Good taste versus the occasional ground-looping jet careening over the edge—it's a trade-off we're willing to make."

THE GYRO-BALL ROLLERHOME LIFESPHERE MARK 1

The pipeline billionaire Rex van Moving is in constant motion, traveling the USA in search of innocent virgin land and the legislators, politicians, and energy czars needed to help grab it in his crusade to crisscross the far reaches of the nation with unsightly metal tubes speeding one or another toxic liquid from under the earth to this or that smoke-belching, chemical-spewing megafactory for conversion into money.

Planes need airports. Limousines are too slow. Even helicopters lack the go-everywhere capabilities Rex van Moving needs to scope out new pipeline pathways. That's why Rex hired a team of ex-Soviet space scientists and engineers, now desperate for paychecks that won't bounce, to design his innovative roaming home-on-the-road mechanical explorer: the Gyro-Ball Rollerhome Lifesphere Mark 1.

"It's basically a giant gyroscopically balanced live-in rolling titanium ball," he unblushingly brags, "totally computerized to always stay upright as it spins and whirls over the landscape at speeds no dumb SUV or boring RV could come close to rivaling."

Powered by a set of booster rockets built for the Soyuz space project and modified for horizontal instead of vertical propulsion, the Gyro-Ball whirls over hill and dale while Rex and the crew, snugly belted to their seats, bask in gyroscopically induced calm. "It rides as smooth as a Lexus," Rex beams, "and no wonder: the controls are manned by a commander and copilot I lured away from the Russian cosmonaut

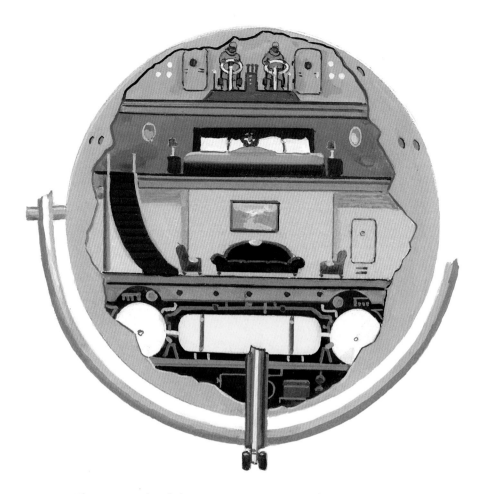

This exquisite hand-drawn cutaway view shows the two-man ex-cosmonaut crew in position in the cockpit of the Lifesphere. One level below in his spacious bedchamber, the lucky owner and sole passenger luxuriates in his sultan-size water bed, facing forward for a panoramic view as the huge silver sphere skips, rolls, and occasionally bounces across the landscape.

Not seen in this view are the gym, TV room, disco, galley, library, smokehouse, and Jacuzzi that help make this not only the first but also the only mobile home to ever host former president Bill Clinton at a 2010 fund-raiser for a fee of less than $100,000. Mr. Clinton stayed just thirty seconds. "How did I know Bubba gets carsick?" moans Rex van Moving.

program with perks like Stoli in the water faucets, fur hats, uniforms, and indoor plumbing."

And Rex can climb down from the command post and relax in a living area featuring a gyroscopic water bed, HD 3-D jumbo-screen porn, and even an onboard Automat that vends his beloved pecan pies and Black Forest cakes.

Because it's not technically either a truck or a car or an airplane or a boat or an earthmover, et cetera, et cetera, the usual government safety and emissions regulations and restrictions don't apply. "In short," grins Rex, "the highway patrol can't touch us." And because it's meant strictly for Rex van Moving's exclusive private use—no freight or flammables or explosives or heavy loads—neither do the rules of interstate commerce bedevil it. "No weigh-station stops for the ol' Gyro-Ball," he preens. "Hell, it don't even need a *license plate!*"

Such freedoms grant the Gyro-Ball license to maraud the interstates, if the mood strikes, at speeds exceeding two hundred miles per hour, an H. G. Wells fantasy sprung to life—to tear through Nebraska cornfields and across Dakota prairies, scouting potential pipeline routes, like some oversize titanium-clad tumbleweed. To skip across the Mississippi or the Colorado like a Brobdingnagian water bug en route to discovering new virgin territory begging to be defiled. And, indeed, to mount the marble steps of any state capitol as easily as it descends, quicker than a Slinky, scattering hapless admirers, or at least frightened onlookers, in its wake.

The normally outspoken van Moving is coy about any plans to place his personal gyro-conveyance into commercial production—though it's now an open secret that the U.S. Department of Defense has shown more than a casual interest. Pentagon scuttlebutt has it that army planners see an obvious role for such a vehicle operating in the Afghan outback, a kind of land-borne drone chasing and crushing militants or anybody and anything else in its path without the annoying publicity.

Perhaps, maybe, could be. Should such a plan go forward, the fact that former vice president Dick Cheney recently joined the van Moving corporate board "can't," as one inside observer says, "hurt."

WORLD'S LONGEST FIREPLACE

A genuine Easter Island stone head, so hauntingly reminiscent of his first wife. Custom-quarried blocks of ancient stone donated from Stonehenge and the Egyptian pyramids and the Great Wall of China—"the donor being yours truly," the proud homeowner beams—went into building the mile-long fireplace that spans the north end of the great room in fire-insurance baron F.F. Formica's Wyoming ranch house.

F.F.'s love of history is exceeded only by his passion for fire—close to a mania, in fact, since he earned a coveted Person of Interest file in the Toledo, Ohio, fire department's investigative unit as a sixteen-year-old. A fixation would blaze into a career; the vast arson-insurance corporation (or "sinister octopus of conspiracy and fraud," as certain commercial rivals whimper) that F.F. founded has since been connected with four-alarm fires of unknown or suspicious origin that have razed a few thousand buildings nationwide. His business career, ironically, was financed by the

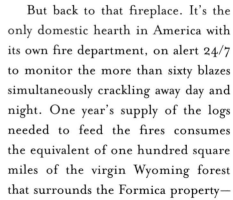

insurance settlement from a fire that burned down his grandmother's cottage. "But I didn't know she was in it," he pleads.

But back to that fireplace. It's the only domestic hearth in America with its own fire department, on alert 24/7 to monitor the more than sixty blazes simultaneously crackling away day and night. One year's supply of the logs needed to feed the fires consumes the equivalent of one hundred square miles of the virgin Wyoming forest that surrounds the Formica property— or used to. "At the rate we're cutting it down," F.F. envisages, "the land around here is pretty soon gonna be as bare as a nudist's bum."

Curiously enough, while F.F. frequently retires to his ranch for Easter and the Fourth of July and Labor Day, he has never celebrated Christmas cozying up to his roaring fire. "Nobody's around at Christmas, and the fire departments are mostly understaffed or off duty, so it's the best time of year to torch a business," he enthuses. "Or so they say."

The Toledo

Today's Weather:
Like yesterday

MONDAY, MARCH 20, 1947 - Final Edition

Local Lad, 16, Tabbed as Fire Dept's Youngest-Ever "Person of interest"

Toledo Chief Acts In Aftermath of Suspicious Blazes

Special To the Blade

TOLEDO, March 19: A West Side boy has been publicly designated "a person of interest" by the Fire Department after several blazes of unknown origin erupted near his neighborhood this week.

One conflagration bued dow a cottage at 34 Sumacn Street – the home of the youth's grandmother, Mrs. Fleagle Formica, a widow. Within two days, fires engulfed a candy store, the boy's father's mattress repair shop, his uncle's tannery, and the 1st National Bank branch a block from the house where he lives with his father, F. F. Formica, and his mother Mrs. Formica.

"We want to keep this little b-----d under constant watch," Toledo Fire Chief Milt Muggery told The Blade. "He asked for a Zippo lighter for a birthday gift when he was three," Chief Muggery revealed. "Came by the firehouse one time, and set

Toledo Teenager F.F. Formica Jr., 16, In a Family Photo

F. F. Formica is captured, literally, in this photo accompanying a 1947 Toledo Blade newspaper article hinting that the teenage pyroprodigy's career had already caught fire. Claiming that he thought the gasoline-filled canister he was found holding at the scene of the conflagration in his grandmother's house contained water and that he had been sprinkling the oily rags in the basement, which he mistook for a bouquet of flowers, "to help out my poor ol' crippled granny," the lad further explained that the Zippo lighter found in his pocket had been a gift from his grandmother, who was teaching him to smoke.

F.F. finds fuel for his wood-devouring fireplace right outside his own door from the vast tracts of virgin forest that surround his western retreat. The tonnage of firewood collected annually could heat the entire nation of Iceland for a century or more, but the wastage is even greater. "I can't resist burning things down," confesses F.F., with something more like a smirk than a sob. "My lumberjack crews sometimes get really pissed off when they're out there sawing and hacking away, and suddenly there's this crackling noise and animals rushing all over the place and somebody sniffs the air and yells 'Fire!' and they have to skedaddle. But science tells us that burned-down forests grow back better than ever. So I may be a pyromaniac, but put down that I'm also a conservationist."

SIR SITH RAM PRAMBA'S "TOP O' THE WORLD"

Certified Nepalese Sherpa guides leading adventurers to the craggy peak of Mount Everest would be a humdrum everyday exercise today—that is if the adventurers weren't in tuxedos and ball gowns and juggling martinis, and the peak of Mount Everest were not perched atop a Park Avenue penthouse.

Slicing off the top of the world's highest mountain and transposing its millions of tons of ancient rock from the Himalayas to the roof of a New York apartment building was a childhood dream of the flamboyant Bangalorean packaged-suttee mogul Sir Sith Ram Pramba. But unlike Sir Sith's other childhood dreams—dating film actress Dame May Whitty, driving two racing cars at once, being voted King of the Gypsies—this one has come true.

Using more dynamite than was expended in the building of the Hoover Dam, the construction of Switzerland's longest under-mountain tunnel, and World Wars I and II, Sir Sith's thousand-man "Team

of Dreamers" engineers, stonemasons, and explosives experts applied almost surgical skills to cut Everest's peak loose from the mountain below so evenly that the site was left as flat and smooth as a tabletop. Pramba doesn't own what's left of Everest, but the hyperimaginative Indian entrepreneur has plans to lease that site and thereupon establish the Himalayan Range's first polo field, once such initial knots as below-zero temperatures, one-hundred-mile-an-hour winds, the impossibility of ever growing grass, and hoisting delicate ponies twenty-two thousand feet up are unkinked.

But back to Everest-on-the-Avenue. At sunset on most days, Sir Sith's guests gather on the terrace of an adjoining penthouse prior to their ascent, for cocktails and canapés and lectures on climbing etiquette by the Sherpa guides ("No snowball throwing please! Thank you for no spray-can graffiti!"), whose overland trek from Kathmandu to Manhattan has left them barely winded; in fact, they're rarin' to climb. And small wonder, since tipping is permitted and

the diminutive human packhorses hope to "clean up," padding annual incomes that vary from one to two cents a year back home.

Environmental Hysteria does swirl around Sir Sith's spectacular slab of rock. The sentimentalists carp about one of the world's great natural monuments having been disfigured for the private pleasure of one selfish magnate. The ecology freaks cavil about the danger of rock slides pelting the street below with giant boulders. The fern-bar quiche-heads bemoan the spending of millions to soothe one man's ego, while prairie dogs suffer from weasel-measles epidemics and Saturday mail delivery goes the way of hootenannies and the Yellow Pages. Will that soaring hunk of Himalayan rock attract vultures and cormorants and other winged vermin that skulk on giddy heights? Has anyone studied the likely climatological effects of a cloud-shrouded mountain peak looming above Manhattan? Is the city in for summer blizzards, gale-force winds, and a rash of falling frozen mountaineers?

Sir Sith Ram Pramba can only shrug while puffing on another Robusto—not so easy a gesture to pull off, actually; not with a brandy snifter in his other hand and a lady friend on his knee. "The rich are very different from you and you and you," he observes, mischievously misquoting F. Scott Fitzgerald. "We have most of the fun. No, make that *all* of the fun."

Mountain climbers suffer superhuman privation for the prize of little more than a fleeting feeling of triumph at reaching the peak. That's not enough for Sir Sith Ram Pramba's ritzy Manhattan pals as they clamber on tiptoe up the transplanted cone of Mount Everest: awaiting them at the summit is Sir Sith's personal valet, Mandrake, who mixes martinis and dishes out hors d'oeuvres. Now that's more like it. Hit me again, Mandrake!

Getting back down Top o' the World after cocktail hour is no breeze. Descending the steep grade without handrails to steady one's way and with one's already shaky sense of balance made woozy by booze—and for ladies in high heels every errant step is an invitation to a suicidal plunge—is not an option. Does one turn and cautiously edge backward down the steep grade on all fours like a bear sliding down a tree trunk? Not only too slow, but too, too embarrassing.

Faithful Mandrake to the rescue. Moments after he autodials a number on his cell phone, hustling up the slope come a crew of Sherpas, who make quick work of hoisting the greenhorn climbers on their backs and sure-footedly half running downhill. And in moments, our grateful friends are milling about the "terrace firma," knocking back fresh martinis and trading shivery tales of peril and final triumph. They have conquered mighty Everest, without spilling a drop.

TRATTORIA AMAZONIA

A five-star outdoor restaurant high atop the leafy Amazonian rain forest—or, let's be accurate, tipsily balanced on the topmost layer of leaves in the leafy Amazonian rain forest—must qualify as at least the eighth wonder of the hospitality world.

"Really," chirps Freddie (no last name, he says, adding that it's too complicated to get into just now), "we had no choice." ("We" being Freddie and his wife, Ditzi.) "When we came here after finishing our project in Rio"—the entrepreneurial couple had imported thousands of cardboard refrigerator cartons and rented them out as houses to budget-conscious families longing to move indoors from the open air, open sewage, and gunplay—"we found there was nowhere to eat between Bahia and the Uruguayan border. So naturally we decided to open the Amazon Basin's only authentic Tuscan restaurant. Made perfect sense, because like everywhere else, gracious living here in Brazil is all about wining and dining. Particularly the wining."

Okay, Freddie and Ditzi, understood—but why locate your house and your restaurant way up in the trees?

"The bugs, the snakes, the monkeys, the locals!" Ditzi makes a face, then another face, then *another* face. "We had to get above all that."

"And besides," adds Freddie, "by going treetop, we saved a bundle: no floor or walls or a roof. Just lay down a carpet, haul up some tables and chairs, and you're open for business!"

The ecological injury of planting a working restaurant smack in the middle of the jungle: the smoke, the greasy kitchen runoff, the garbage dumped in the river, the slaughterhouse for veal calves and resulting offal effluvia seeping into the water table—not to mention the disposal system for the restaurant's chemical latrines, i.e., emptying accumulated waste matter with a cry of "Look out below!"—has raised the ire of innumerable do-gooder environmental worrywarts around the world. "But it's nothing a few hundred comped meals for my pal the local police chief, and the local governor, and the army, plus a few folks over in Brasília, can't calm down," Freddie winks.

A hundred-and-forty-foot rope ladder is the sole means of access to Trattoria Amazonia for patrons arriving on the riverbank below via motor launch or dugout canoe. "Only a handful of guests who made reservations have failed to show up," crows Freddie, "and we haven't entirely given up hope of finding them yet. I mean, even the natives go missing all the time down there in that endless green hell of jaguars and boa constrictors and, of course, those bare-naked Amazonians with their blowguns and poison darts and their goddamn iPods."

Those who make it up to restaurant level to feast on the Amazon Basin's finest cuisine must first pass through Ditzi's boutique, Savage Chic, where Amazonian bric-a-brac like shrunken human heads and live man-eating snakes are for sale. The trattoria's meals are prepared in an outdoor kitchen nestled in the foliage directly beneath. "The waitstaff are all local orphan kids, super agile," Freddie notes. "Oh, they still drop a lot of plates and glasses and bottles clambering up topside from the kitchen through that maze of branches while trying to balance their serving trays. Frankly, we'd be frosted if we were paying them, but what the hell, they're working just for all the leftovers they can eat."

Isn't the employment of minors without paying them illegal, even in notoriously lax Brazilian law? "Hey, numbnuts," Freddie barks, "we came down here because only one law applies. The law of the jungle."

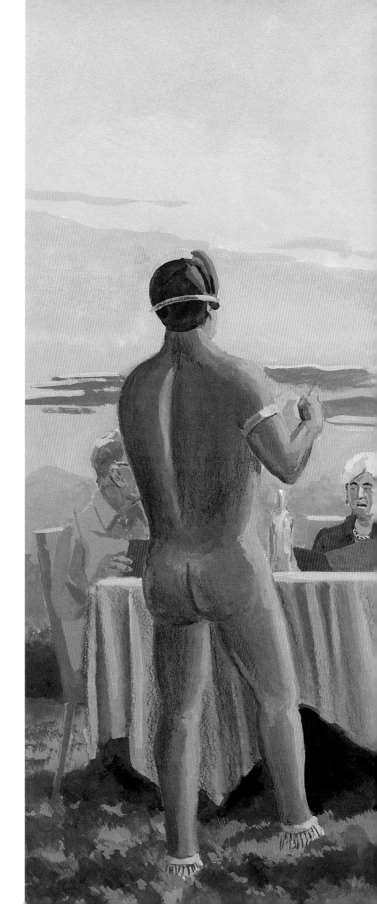

An authentic absence of restrooms, an authentic absence of air-conditioning, authentically naked Amazonian waiters—that's what Ditzi decreed to ensure a true Amazon jungle experience for her Trattoria Amazonia patrons.

"Those native Amazonian waiters of ours don't speak a word of English," trills our hostess/owner, "and what an advantage that is. Makes ordering a no-brainer matter of just checking the box beside the meal you want and handing it over. Saves so much time bickering over details."

Commendable integrity, but how does such strict insistence on authenticity square with an alleged "trattoria" whose menu lists not a single dish Italiano amid its Beef 'n' Cheeseburgers, Peking Fried Duck, and Donuts à la Dunkin' as a dessert? "Don't nitpick," says our hyper but also hypersensitive hostess/owner/table captain. "Might as well ask what's an Italian restaurant doing in the middle of Central Nowhere, Brazil!

"This project is all about us, not them," she explains, cocking a thumb at the diners struggling to keep their balance while swaying in their chairs, which are swaying in turn on a floor that is a mere flimsy carapace of leaves and branches, themselves swaying in the evening breeze. "We eat indoors at home and not out there with the flying bugs and mosquitoes and buzzards that'll grab a burger right off your plate if you don't bring your shotgun. And then there's those sudden downpours around sunset. You crazy?

"If you do come here to eat," says our enchanting hostess/owner/table captain/cashier, "you eat the grub we like. 'Trattoria' sounds more Brazilian than, say, 'diner.' Don't know what the Brazilian word for 'restaurant' is. Probably 'el dumpo,' if you catch my drift. As for the food, we're Americans all the way, raised on government-inspected meat and chemically enhanced white bread and instant potatoes. So if you want to eat monkey brains and rat steaks like the natives, be our guest. Get down there to ground level and start rooting.

"We close at sundown, sharp, and not a minute later," coos our charming owner/hostess/table captain/cashier/maître d'. "Jaguars are nocturnal hunters, you know. And Jesus, can they climb trees!"

THROUGH THE REDWOODS, FROM THE INSIDE

Northern California's mighty giant redwood trees are a rare ecological and historical treasure," reverently intones San Francisco playboy/rakehell/Hotspur/avid stamp collector Fox Hunt XV, the heir to so many fortunes his iPad exploded trying to keep track of them all. "The redwoods are a precious American heritage, like Justin Bieber," marvels Fox, "even though he's Canadian. Just being around them makes you feel closer to God. Or to some VIP way up there.

"That's why I had my crew get in there while the Sierra Club wasn't looking and chop a few dozen of those big beauties down, then hollow them out and haul them to a flat spot where they could be laid end to end—creating the first section of the Fox Hunt Transcontinental Private No-Trespassing One-Way All-Redwood Tunnel."

You heard right: a veritable three-thousand-mile-long tube twenty feet in diameter, weatherproof and cop-proof, toll-free and free of traffic, bored and hacked from some of the oldest wood on earth and running straight through from San Francisco to New York City. "It's going to make the giant redwoods so famous that it wouldn't surprise me if folks from Nebraska to Iowa and, who knows, all three Dakotas start growing their own," says Fox. "And *I'll* be even more famous as the only man in the world licensed to drive in the world's only indoor superhighway. PS, I'm the one issuing the licenses.

"I figure I'll make it across the continent in a day and a half max," Fox Hunt XV predicts, "unless I want to stop at a strip club or a casino or some

Crack five-man crews are posted at stations along the tunnel's entire coast-to-coast route, spaced at two-hundred-mile intervals. This cutaway illustration shows Station 128, near Pottstown, Pennsylvania, as the crew rushes to change tires, check the oil, wipe the windshield, pump in fuel from an overhead exterior tank, and alertly step aside if the driver needs to use his private restroom, where the attendant waits to brush him off and hand him a towel and to provide stay-awake stimulants from mild to psychedelic if unobserved.

Inspectors guided by flashlights are constantly walking the tunnel from end to end in search of discarded bottles and live cigar butts, bark shards, and tire-puncturing splinters from the redwood-plank floor. The nature of tunnel traffic, with the car moving at speeds up to one hundred miles per hour in the creepy dark and with scant time to move aside before the helpless inspector is overtaken (talk about a deer in the headlights!) and flattened like a crêpe suzette, has been calculated by insurance underwriters as posing a threat to life and limb no worse than falling from a twenty-story building.

Fox Hunt XV streaks through his tunnel exclusively in one of his rich collection of closed luxury and high-performance coupes. "My tunnel is outstanding, the one downside being it's a goddamn Waldorf for half the bats in the country," he shivers. "You've got a bottle of Jack in one hand and a Cohiba in the other and a finger on the wheel and you're howling along with the tach needle on the redline, and one of those little bastards swoops by and gets tangled in your hair—it happened once, and fighting it off cost me one of my favorite Bugattis. Plus the pain and expense of that regimen of rabies shots. Brrr!"

other cultural event along the route; I've got an app on my smartphone to keep me updated. Then, once I reach the New York exit, I'll go down to the pier and pick up a new Lambo or something just off the boat from Europe, switch cars, maybe look up a few gal-pals and take in *The Lion King*—I've seen that show a hundred times—then order takeout from Daniel or someplace, get in the car, and it's pedal to the metal all the way home."

To ease the going, the tunnel is ingeniously furnished with a continuous driver's-side shelf at window level, so Fox can scoop up snacks, smokes, fifths of Wild Turkey, and other travel necessities almost without slowing down. That's his prized classic 1954 Bentley Continental in the picture, but the speed-minded Hunt can choose from a vast stable of ultrathirsty, ultra-high-performance coupes, which are refueled at pumps strung every hundred miles along the tunnel's entire length.

It's the only U.S. superhighway fragrant with the mellow aroma of aged wood, the only windowless three-thousand-mile-long structure anywhere—the superlatives just keep piling up. Which Fox Hunt XV could himself be doing if he keeps forgetting to turn on his headlights.

The redwood tunnel crosses the Mississippi River at one of its narrowest points, in Minnesota, en route from the West to East coasts—or East to West coasts, depending on the direction being driven in this strictly one-way indoor thoroughfare.

Since no regulations exist on how far aboveground a nonsubterranean tunnel must be, important savings were realized by not sinking the redwood tunnel below the water or hoisting it bridgelike on pillars, but simply laying it at ground level between the riverbanks. The clearance for river traffic is less than ten feet and hardly a day goes by that some unsuspecting pleasure boat or barge— despite the clearly displayed warning—smashes prow-first into the tunnel.

Happily, so sturdy is the trunk of the mighty redwood that no damage is ever inflicted, inside or out; tunnel workers patrolling the roadway report only a faint bumping sound and a mild momentary shaking.

PAINTING
A RIVER PUCE

Colored water is as old as Kool-Aid, but a whole fast-moving river primed to change color at the flick of a switch? Pharmaceutical patent fixer Otis McSunnyworth wanted something not store-bought or in any way predictable to surprise his new bride, Voluptua—the only former groin model to market her own line of eco-friendly sex toys—with as a high school graduation gift.

"Voluptua was all about color," marvels Otis. "Always said it was so cool that everything in the world was a color. So I figured, why does this ultraviolet gal have to sit there looking out at the same-old, some-old muddy green and brown water rushing by? Why can't I surprise and astonish her—she who, one, loves color so much and, two, needs cheering up what with all the medication?

"So what I thought up," he explains, "was two chemical storage tanks, one on either bank of the Big Wet Rat River that flows right past the deck of our AAA-frame fishing lodge, and then bridge them with a high-pressure forty-four-spigot tube running right over the river below.

"I hired a color consultant straight from the Benjamin Moore mixing labs," McSunnyworth recounts. "Standing there at the control console on the deck of my lodge, that guy can—just by twirling a dial—computer-mix the chemicals in the tank to create the exact color I ask for, turn on the spigots, and release the result into the river, changing it in seconds, like magic, to puce, fuchsia, heliotrope—any color Voluptua

might choose to complement the outfit she's wearing at the moment or her postoverdose mood.

"And, while I'm not a bragging type of man," Otis brags, "I hired one of those water-bombing flying boats from out in British Columbia to come in real low and unload a ton of those teeny-weeny glitter flakes, like at kids' parties? Mix that stuff with the paint and the river doesn't know what hit it, but a certain gal in a bikini holding a martini, she does. Or did."

The color riot on the Big Wet Rat River does have its critics, in the form of local environmentalists and the folks who have lived on its shores for decades. "But after they found out that the chemicals we use to tint the water kill all the fish and anybody can go in and scoop 'em up for free," says Otis, "they thought different."

But all of Otis's enterprise and money went for naught. The marriage and the happy notion of coloring the Big Wet Rat River have ended; Voluptua suddenly left him for her gluten-free Rosicrucian astrological coach just two days before Otis could unveil her surprise graduation gift, seriously denting his congenital optimism. "All that effort, all that money, all that love down the metaphorical drain," he mutters. "Might just as well have married some color-blind dumb-dumb."

Here are four vivid examples of the Big Wet Rat River's almost infinite palette of colors, courtesy of modern chemical science and split-second timing by the supervisor of mixing and his crew at their post on the catwalk connecting the twin paint vats.

Matching the exact hue of Voluptua's bikinis in the swift-moving river at the touch of a button required a technological outlay estimated at twice that expended in celebrating North Korean midget and party animal Kim Jong-un's tenth high school reunion. "Of course those clowns spend money like water on their entertainment," Otis notes, "so that's just a conservative estimate."

Almost overlooked in the Environmental Protection Agency's official complaint is the importance to the overall color effect of the billions of flecks of glitter cascaded down to mix with those rich reds, yellows, puces, mauves, and heliotropes. Let go like a rush of sugar from an overturned bowl from the belly of a flying boat normally used to douse forest fires, the glitter creates a twinkling extra dimension as it joins the swirling Big Wet Rat on its pell-mell journey downstream. That glitter has been found in the bellies of fish as far away as the South China Sea and Iceland. "That makes me world famous," Otis beams. "So spending all that money losing that little hoyden—it was worth it!"

TAJ MAHAL HAUNTS SILICON VALLEY, AND VICE VERSA

What does a seventeen-year-old Silicon Valley billionaire who has everything need most?

"Space!" retorts Clarence Drooley, a megageek so smart he can read upside down while blindfolded. Nixing the palace at Versailles as too showy, Clarence went on a global shopping tour before deciding on India's fabled Taj Mahal palace, constructed in the city of Agra in Uttar Pradesh in the mid-1600s. He had its family mausoleum desanctified, dismantled, and reassembled at the five-thousand-acre Los Gatos tract where he lives in an Airstream trailer. "Yeah, I heard people were pissed at me for busting up and shipping away their coolest building," Clarence says. "But money talks and have-nots walk."

India's "impoverished" millions elicit scant sympathy, and certainly no money, from the tightfisted Drooley—tightfisted on principle. "Didn't they read *Atlas Shrugged*?" he barks. "Ayn Rand got it right. Only suckers help people less fortunate than themselves. I'm even teaching my dog—name of Howard Roark, ever read

The Fountainhead?—to be less dependent on me, to break him of expecting handouts like food. He's becoming the world's first Objectivist canine. Too bad dogs can't read—if they could, those do-gooder charity pounds would be empty."

The sole occupant of the renamed Taj Me-All (a cryptic tribute to Ms. Rand), the reclusive Drooley lives with Howard Roark in only one room, an elaborately paneled outer chamber with eighty-two-foot-high ceilings just down the hall from the Taj's centerpiece twin catafalques. "Those coffins give me the creeps," admits Clarence. "I might sell them back to the family and get them the hell out of here. Four-hundred-year-old strangers—what a downer."

The ascetic prodigy owns a sleeping bag, a trail bike, and little else. He receives no guests, passing most days playing Xbox and ordering takeout so he doesn't have to employ a chef or waitstaff whom he'd need to talk to.

"I *could* have my mom come in to clean and cook," he ponders. "But she couldn't solve Fermat's Last Theorem if she had a whole day to do it in."

HUCKSTER FRUNK JR. SR.'S DREAM TEPEE

What does a rabid fan of both the Nez Perce Native American tribe *and* speedboats dream about? Hmm. If he's the multibillionaire ex–Department of Native American Affairs Casino Graft Director Huckster Frunk Jr. Sr., and you absolutely *must* know, it's Native Americans driving speedboats.

But Huckster did more than lie around dreaming. He designed and built an ultra-high-tech high-speed motor vessel surmounted by a five-story Nez Perce tepee, playfully named *Xanadu* "because 'Xanadu' sounds just like the way somebody with a heavy Hungarian accent would say 'Canada,'" Huckster explains.

He may or may not be kidding about that, but Huckster Frunk is dead serious about pursuing his dual hobby. It begins with *Xanadu*'s four mighty one-thousand-horsepower Pratt & Whitney aircraft engines bolted to the four corners of a supporting platform mounted on pontoons. Revved up to full speed, their propeller blades generate enough power to propel the five-ton vessel over the water at speeds of forty to fifty miles per hour—preceded by a dramatic ceremonial fleet of Nez Perce–inspired war canoes. The "braves" brandishing their paddles are another Frunk innovation: electronically guided robots capable of obeying word commands. "It's fun to yell 'Go scalp those gawking tourists in their stupid little Sunfish!' in Nez Perce," Huckster chuckles.

Xanadu may be the tallest tepee ever constructed, and it is definitely the only one with a lightweight frame of molybdenum and aluminum rings made in Friedrichshafen, Germany, by descendants of the skilled workmen who built the zeppelin *Hindenburg.* Then Mrs. Frunk took charge of the exterior covering, a mylar-asbestos blend sewn together by skilled Nez Perce squaws using a traditional time-honored method—binding the seams so tightly that not even a blunt tomahawk blow could sever them. But the authenticity doesn't carry over to the usual exterior decoration of Nez Perce symbols. "Those wouldn't work," Huckster Frunk huffs. "The Nez Perce worship the sun and stars and bears and crap. We worship different gods." Thus the Dolce & Gabbana, Rolex, Dior, Fendi, and a riot of other upscale logos honoring the more down-to-earth deities that guide the Frunks through life and the Rue de la Paix.

Plying the far-western waterways and sticking to the Missouri, the Yellowstone, and other wide rivers, the *Xanadu* is credited with scaring away most of the birdlife with its earsplitting engine noise while mangling the rest in its razor-sharp spinning blades. Marine life is said to be endangered by the thick flow of leaking aviation fuel streaming astern. Riverside wildlife has been "taking it on the chin, the belly, the head, the haunches, and nearly everywhere else," one forest ranger has testified, "from machine-gun bursts originating from the *Xanadu* during frequent antipirate defensive exercises." Indeed, the *Xanadu* has been listed in the Sierra Club's Ten Most Disgusting Threats to Nature list for a record sixty-two months running.

Do the Frunks pause on their voyages long enough to invite their Nez Perce heroes aboard for a powwow and a peace pipe? "You must be kidding."

This beautifully detailed artist's sketch shows one of the world's only all-electronic Nez Perce braves that precede the *Xanadu* on all expeditions in a trailblazing advance canoe party.

Each four-hundred-pound, thirty-five-million-dollar device stands six feet six inches tall and features fully extensible arms and legs with a 360-degree range of movement in the elbows and knees. It can hurl a spear with 87 percent accuracy at targets up to one thousand feet away. Meanwhile, its 120 Intel transistors activate behaviors such as vigorous head shaking and tomahawk wielding with the lightest touch of the color-coded keys on a handheld control pad.

Maximum paddling capacity is thirty miles per hour for thirty hours without recharging. A built-in stereo "voice" carries up to a distance of four thousand feet and can articulate more than one hundred commands, including "Coming through!" and "The U.S. Cavalry sucks!" in Nez Perce, Crow, Paiute, English, and Latin.

SCHUSSING THE AVALANCHE IN YOUR OWN SKI LODGE

The fastest ranch in Idaho, the world's first fully enclosed toboggan, the biggest sled ever built—you name it, El Rancho Avalancho fits the bill. And by any name it's meant to harness Mother Nature's fury for hair-raising downhill plunges, powered by nothing but gravity and a few million tons of fast-moving snow.

Owner Jack K. Spratt, he of the Spratt Savings & Usury empire, is the brains behind this bold new concept in megabillionaire western recreational mayhem, launched from a high plateau in front of the earthbound Spratt Mansion atop Spratt Gorge, a deep gouge in the earth dynamited into being from what used to be Spratt Mountain.

It was born of a simple yet profound Spratt observation: "I was staring out the living-room window one day," Jack recalls, "when it hit me like—well, like an avalanche. God didn't make all those steep mountainsides only for skiers and tobogganers and snowboarders. Nowhere is it written in the Good Book that you can't go bucketing down in a house!

On the other hand, I suppose you could rightly ask what those old-time Arabs knew about mountains and avalanches or, Christ, snow!"

The way to achieve his quasibiblical vision came in another landslide of insight. Jack up a multilevel contemporary ski chalet and slide a set of sturdy metal runners underneath, shove it to the edge of a steep incline, and get set for the ride of your life.

To get a large dwelling with walk-in fireplaces, saunas, and a complete French Country kitchen to move downhill, Jack K. Spratt realized, you can't just shove off like a skier. "You need an avalanche," he advises, "to overcome the inertia and get her up to speed fast. So we start by tucking explosive charges into the snow mass all around the rancho.

"The second you light the fuse," he continues, "the snow explodes and starts pushing El Rancho Avalancho downhill. The snow gathers volume and momentum fast, uprooting every tree and boulder in its path.

"It's blinding white looking out from the picture windows," Jack exults, "snow swirling like a tornado and the place shaking and rocking amid a deafening roar. There goes the chandelier! Chairs and sofas and beds rolling all over the place, window glass shattering, wine cellar's now in the rumpus room, and where's the dog? Pure absolute chaos, pure absolute fun!"

Suggestion: what about seat belts for the inhabitants to try to minimize the physical toll of life in a runaway house?

"Hey," Jack K. Spratt snarls, "it wasn't pantywaists who settled the West. Study the literature, check the old photos. You'll find that no consarned cowpoke ever wore a goldang seat belt!"

In this stunning live-action series of paintings, our artist catches a Western Snow Mole, classified as an endangered rodent, scuttling directly into the path of the prototype El Rancho Avalancho ski lodge as it hurtles down a mountainside on a test run. The pilot applied full braking power, which triggered a perfect somersault of the ski lodge before it made a perfect landing and continued on its downward course. The squashed remains of the Snow Mole were turned over to a taxidermist; fully restored to lifelike form, it now adorns the mantelpiece in the great room of the current El Rancho Avalancho lodge. Because it could not be proven that the prototype actually crushed the tiny animal—the painting being disallowed as reliable proof—the $50 fine for destroying a member of an endangered species was never paid.

LOOK UPON MY BISON, YE MIGHTY, AND DESPAIR

I was diagnosed with what the docs call 'incurable acute egomania' when I was a toddler," confessed billionaire Hollywood-cemetery-owner-turned-Wyoming-ranch-owner Sid Z. Sidney. "I don't just want to stand out, I *need* to stand out."

That confronted Sid with a problem after he'd purchased his vast new spread, cheek by jowl with all those other plutocrats' vast spreads. "The far West turns folks into bigness nuts," he observes, "always bragging 'I got the biggest spread,' 'I got the biggest bunkhouse,' 'My new wife's got the biggest jugs.' So I knew if I was gonna stand out, I had to get famous for something *big*.

"And there it was, right in front of me," he recalls. "None of those show-offs ever thought about the bison, for God's sake! The most attention-getting thing about the West! So I decided Sidney Z. Sidney would be famous for having the biggest goddamn bison in Wyoming. In the West. In the world. Not just big-bison big. I'm talking *big huge ginormous bison big!*"

Breeding a truly jumbo-size bison by conventionally incremental means, generation after generation, could take years if not decades. Too slow for Sid. Luck again smiled on him, as it has throughout a long and charmed life: through his Nazi SS Death's Head Sturmtruppen reenactment club, he heard tell of a secretive eugenicist, an elderly German emigrant breeding mile-long snakes and vulture-size hummingbirds in his adopted Paraguayan jungle homeland. "One of his ancestors was Mary Shelley's model for Frankenstein," Sid recounts. "He once took a long submarine ride and he still gives himself a

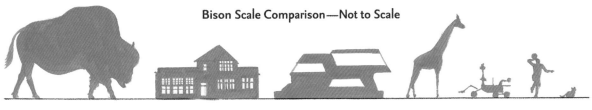

Bison Scale Comparison—Not to Scale

Stalin's Dacha   Houseboat   Giraffe   Mars Explorer   NBA star   Cat

Patron Sidney Z. Sidney shields ninety-five-year-old Doctor X, father of the Brobdingnagian bison, from the nosy media pack as they make a run for the rear entrance of the airport terminal near Sidney's ranch. The formerly licensed physician and medical experimenter, now a wizard of cloning, has finished his American mission and is being whisked to the chartered flight that will return him to his Paraguayan jungle cabin-cum-retreat-cum-hideaway without the hassle of passing through U.S. Customs. Frail, speaking almost no English, and pathologically averse to being photographed, the tense and temperamental Doctor X spit on a reporter and kicked a fotog just after this picture was painted.

"Jetzt ich muss ein anderer facelift haben!" he was heard to mutter, in what sounded like Pennsylvania Dutch. "Scheisse! Doppel scheisse!"

shot every day for his claustrophobia. That's all anybody knows for sure. He gives his name as just Doctor X!"

Utilizing an entrepreneurial mix of cash, an artist pal to create a legal-looking new passport and visa, and a still hush-hush stratagem to distract Interpol, Sid lured what he termed the "almost criminally shy" scientist out of Paraguay and set him up with his own lab on his ranch. And within the year, after long weeks and months of experimentation—punctuated by spine-tingling howls and loud thumping and crashing sounds in the night—"Frankenbuff," as Sid dubbed him, stumbled out into the daylight. A perfectly proportioned male bison taller than a three-story house, tipping the scales on the far side of twenty tons and strong enough to bunt a Trailways bus into the next county. A herd of similar four-footed behemoths would soon follow from the anonymous genius's virtual-animal assembly line.

"I don't know how he did it and I don't care," Sid snaps. "It's made me Big Man Number One on the prairie and that's what counts." There are issues: the herd has to be grouped in small numbers, miles apart, because when they gallop over the landscape en masse, they trigger earthquakes. One dark night a low-flying plane bounced off a bull; flashing red lights may need to be mounted on the backs of all of Sid's bison to prevent a repeat. Sid is currently consulting with the Federal Bureau of Prisons about building a wall around his spread, high enough and stout enough to contain a charging Frankenbuff.

Sid sees even more fame coming out of his bold experiment one day. "You got any idea how much manure one normal-size bison generates in a day?" he asks, rhetorically. "Well, multiply that by the manure my herd generates in a month. Multiply those months by whatever. Point is, pretty soon there'll be enough bison shit to build the tallest goddamn mountain in Wyoming. And I'll be famous all over again!"

AZTEC TEMPLE, TWENTY-FIRST-CENTURY TEMPO

Delicia and Thor Glut, self-confessed "history nuts," shelled out millions of her inheritance money (she's the granddaughter of Hobart Glut, the noted Appalachian "Black-Lung King") to purchase a newly unearthed Aztec temple in Mexico's historic Peninsula of the Tortured Dead—the very day their astrology coach revealed that the birth chart of the legendary Aztec king Itzcoatl, who may have built it, was chillingly similar to those of Candy's and Randy's, their two pugs.

"We wanted to name the place in Itzcoatl's honor," Thor says, "but, frankly, ugh—that moniker sounds like somebody being strangled. And anyhow, nobody can spell or even pronounce it, so we just settled on Dunroamin. Which is also the name of our yacht."

It's a year-round leisure paradise for the Gluts, but weekends are when Dunroamin comes most alive. That's when Delicia and Thor turn their beloved ancient ruin into a roaring circus of automotive mayhem, flying in pals from as far away as Texas and Louisiana for the sole purpose of forcing them—under the half-jesting, half-dead-serious threat of no cocaine after dinner—to belt themselves in and accelerate one or another of the couple's stable of powerful sports cars up one set of temple steps, through the temple itself, and down the steps on the other side. "The Aztec Two-Hundred-Step, we call it," jokes Thor, limping only when he tries to walk, the aftereffect of a recent crash-landing in a Lamborghini with a stuck throttle.

The temple takes a terrible beating from the repeated effects of out-of-control cars colliding with stone, infuriating the historic preservation nuts kept safely outside the surrounding electrified fence, but not as much as the cars do, and certainly not as much as the drivers do, since few of them are skilled at piloting six-hundred-horsepower vehicles on stomach-turning near-vertical suicide charges up one hundred steps and almost instantaneously

Those flickering pitch torches are gas jets, perhaps the sole unauthentic aspect of the sacred ancient Aztec sacrifice ceremony that unfolds après Sunday dinner. Mounting the priest's rostrum overlooking the circular sacrifice pit, both hands stuffed with crisp new U.S. hundred-dollar bills, Delicia beseeches the Aztec deities with a sacred chant, her own lyrics substituting for what she terms "Aztec gobbledygook," sung a cappella to the tune of Neil Diamond's immortal "Sweet Caroline":

Aztec's my game
And my heart is full of love.
I think you're great!
Hope you see me from Above.
Bills, lots of bills . . . thrills,
lots of thrills.
Aztec's my game
Etc. etc. etc.

Delicia then hurls her fistfuls of moola into the pit, where tongues of flame instantly turn them into a carpet of black ash. The Aztec gods have been appeased—or, as Delicia says, "They damn well ought to be." She stands stock-still, pondering the unknowable ("which for Delicia covers a lot of ground," says her hubby) and imbibing the spirit of Holy Communion in the gathering darkness, until the mosquitoes start biting and a voice rolls across the greensward: "Hey, honey, get in here! That *Real Housewives of Beverly Hills* rerun is starting!"

down the one hundred steps on the other side, pedal to the metal—even when sober.

But the indisputable highlight of a Dunroamin weekend comes Sunday evening after the clearing of the wreckage and an early take-out Chinese dinner, when Delicia and Thor and their guests gather before the Pit of Life, designed by Thor after he read about Aztec rituals of human sacrifice in a comic book. Instead of humans, Delicia and Thor toss crisp new bills of U.S. currency into the flames of the pit. "It's a holy moment," Delicia says reverently, "an offering to the gods to ward off Montezuma's revenge and other Mesoamerican evils."

"The bills flutter in the sunset air," Thor adds, "and we all feel at one with nature and the ages and all those dead Aztec folks. The sacrifice is a small price to pay for divine protection from all stomach distress. Well, that and, of course, drinking only bottled water."

AN ARTIFICIAL ICEBERG WON'T MELT, CRUMBLE, OR SINK

Cheap polystyrene ski boots, cheap polystyrene suitcases, cheap polystyrene igloos—clever products for dumb people, an age-old formula for Croesus-type wealth. But a polystyrene *iceberg*? Only the Canadian Styrofoam billionaire Claude Ste. Nervous would—could—conceive of a huge artificial snow-white mountain spun from petroleum byproducts serenely drifting through the Arctic waters. No calving, no rotting, no melting come spring. (Take that, all you global-warming hysterics!) A *motorized* iceberg, honeycombed with salons and bedroom suites and secret chambers enough to embarrass Mad Ludwig's Bavarian castle.

Welcome, in brief, to Claude Ste. Nervous's dream vacation home. Although there's nothing brief about it—from the time it takes to get there (by flying from Montreal to the coast of Baffin Island to hop into the copter that ferries you to the tiny offshore islet where the icebreaker waits to ply the last hundred miles of Arctic sea to the iceberg) to the lazy nature of three-month voyages to nowhere that are the Nervous vacation norm to those voyages' endless twenty-four-hour days of holiday summer sunshine.

While guests loll and sunbathe on his iceberg's sundeck, Claude will often unchain his prized male polar bear, Carmichael, and lead him down to the polystyrene ice floe tied alongside—powered by twin Evinrudes faster than the fastest ocean current—and ride him bareback while spear-hunting baby seals, baby walruses, and baby whales. "I haven't actually got one yet," he confesses, "but I'm not a guy who

Through the magic of patented advanced injection-molding techniques, the interior of the all-polystyrene Ste. Nervous iceberg-cum-floating-palace is honeycombed with chambers, suites, anterooms, and this open reception area giving out onto the main sundeck. No fancy decorator needed: the space welcomes guests with a haunting display of dead Arctic wildlife personally executed by our host. His creative consultant and hair-care director, Miss Kitti Katz, shown here in Arctic mink at the top of the world's only all-Styrofoam spiral staircase with Mr. Ste. Nervous, her inseparable boss, companion, and spiritual coach. (Eco-worrywarts: those baby seals lolling around on the sundeck are very much alive— for now.) Whereas an actual iceberg would be too frigid for sunbathing, sport shooting, and tossing beer cans into the surrounding waters, this sundeck, made of pure petroleum byproducts and chemicals not found in nature, boasts a heated floor and is impervious to cold and almost everything else; in fact, experts predict that it and the entire Styrofoam structure will still be floating around somewhere, indestructible and nonbiodegradable, long after the last iceberg has melted away.

gives up easily, or I'd never have pursued the idea of molding a three-hundred-ton iceberg out of petroleum byproducts in the first place."

The berg is tethered to thirty two-ton underwater lead bars to minimize rolling in high seas or capsizing in a storm, but mostly to stay upright. "Even thirty tons of Styrofoam is light," Claude points out, "but as a grizzled mariner, I've learned that waves can be heavy."

A fleet of polystyrene icebergs isn't beyond the realm of possibility, not with Claude's reflexive zeal to make a buck, but—and it's a big but—he shudders at the idea of unwanted interlopers disturbing his peaceful calm. "I suppose I could build a big polystyrene zeppelin and bomb the goddamn nuisances," he muses. "But that's another thing about polystyrene," he frowns. "It doesn't sink."

Claude Ste. Nervous goes to inordinate lengths to entertain the guests aboard his floating Styrofoam-palace-cum-iceberg. Indeed, he sent a group of Baffin Island Inuit all the way to Hawaii to learn the infectious music of that happy South Seas island folk so that when they had mastered the slack-key guitar and the mandolin and the ukulele, they could return and provide cocktail-hour serenades, making the barren Arctic— if only for an hour or two—a tropical paradise.

But Mr. Ste. Nervous is the first one to admit that not all his bold ideas pan out. "Those guys just aren't very good," he shrugs. "And I find I don't really like the music all that much. A little bit of that Hawaiian umma-umma goes a long way." His ingenious solution: put the Royal Eskimo Hawaiian Serenaders in a boat and place the boat a goodly distance from the Styrofoam-palace-cum-iceberg, where their music can barely be heard.

"Not an ideal solution," Claude admits. "But I couldn't fire these guys. Where else in the straits of Baffinland is a Hawaiian band going to find any work?"

THE ROYAL AND ANCIENT GALAPAGOLF

A natural haven for rare flora and fauna that is absent of predators and human intrusion, a delicate and Edenistic ecosystem duplicated nowhere else on earth—Moe and Madge Flux set foot on the exotic Galapagos Islands off the west coast of South America and instantly came to the same conclusion. "The perfect spot for a miniature golf course!" the couple chimed in unison.

Their chain of minigolf enterprises across North America had made Moe and Madge wealthy; founding a new paradise of ramps, loop-the-loops, fake vegetation, and crappy lawn ornaments where no duffer had ever whiffed a shot before promised to lift the Fluxes into the magical realm of the obscenely rich.

The simple secret? Snob appeal. "Exclusivity had always been missing from miniature golf," confides Moe, "and it held the sport back. No fancy clubs, no championship tournaments on network TV, no Tiger Woods–type stars. But the Royal and Ancient Galapagolf—and tell your lawyer that Galapagolf's a registered service mark of MoeMadge Leisure Industries PLC—changed everything overnight."

A membership in the Royal and Ancient Galapagolf will set you back fifty thousand dollars U.S., plus another ten thousand on remittance to keep Moe and Madge from blackballing you for the first year. Course rules are unique and so strict that violators must pay one hundred dollars cash each to have an offense erased from the scorecard. (Caddies serve triple duty as club luggers, cashiers, and erasers.) For example, it's against the rules to put a ball in play when it's on the ground; the golfer must find some other solid horizontal or semisolid, semihorizontal surface. "Most of the rules are zany shit," Moe admits, "but it adds to the fun. And miniature golf is all about fun. Fun being Madge and me finally getting that *petit trianon* next to a golf course at Cap d'Antibes."

Galapagolfers can expect to play not just around but on or with giant tortoises, blue-footed boobies, seals, and numerous other novelties found at no other miniature golf course in the world. "They just stand around looking dopey and bored," Madge observes, "so why not break up their day? And interacting with humans teaches these ignorant critters what bastards we can be."

Just as no profanity is tolerated on the finer American courses and a dress code is strictly enforced, the Royal and Ancient Galapagolf tolerates no nonalcoholic beverages on the tees and clamps a tight lid on not wagering.

CHARLES DARWIN LAWN JOCKEY
The late, great naturalist loves being outdoors 24/7 now that he's cast in fireproof double-ply Plasticrete that has no natural predators!

"SURVIVAL OF THE SMARTEST" EXER-CAGE
Outsmart the fittest by letting authentic nineteenth-century steam power do all the work while dummy levers make it look like you are!

GALAPAGIFTS

HMS *BEAGLE* POOL RAFT
An inflatable reproduction of
Darwin's favorite cruise ship—
floats in circles until Junior runs it
aground or abandons the voyage!

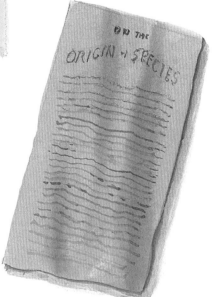

DRINKING BLUE-FOOTED BOOBY
An instant party hit! Weird bird
of the Galapagos dips his beak in
a glass (not included). Not a toy!

GALAPACAT LITTERBOX
Realistic setting includes actual
Galapagos sand—kitty can do his duty
behind the hills for total privacy!

ON THE ORIGIN OF SPECIES
BEACH TOWEL
Complete text of Darwin's 1859
blockbuster best seller is printed
on three-by-six-foot terry-cloth
towels. Order the 120-towel
set to read the entire book.
Magnifying glass suggested!

63

Moe and Madge bring their own unique sensibility and personal touch to every aspect of the Galapagolf complex. The miniature course's par-27 Leaning Tower of Pisa sixteenth hole is pure sentiment, meant to evoke the 1975 Italian honeymoon the Fluxes came that close to taking with a plastic and plywood model of the famed Risorgimento skyscraper, complete with distinctive tilt, set offshore a quarter-mile distant from the tee atop a rock outcropping.

And the par-2 ninth hole, a homemade scale replica of Moe's beloved Yankee Stadium in New York City, his "second home," which he hopes to one day visit.

That seemingly easy ninth hole poses a pesky Galapachallenge to even a championship-level Galapagolfer, largely because those ubiquitous giant lizards that hang around sunning themselves tend to dart out with lightning speed to snatch up errant golf balls as they're chipped into the stadium, and scuttle away. It's perhaps less a case of innocent reptile hijinks than cold-blooded human commerce; the Equadorian FBI openly suspects the lizards have been drilled to pluck up those pricey Kro-Flites with their forked tongues and cough them up to their trainer—tentatively identified as either Moe or Madge, or both—for resale.

"A total misunderstanding," huffs Moe. "We want our Galapaguests to enjoy a maximum entertaining experience. Those golf balls aren't stolen, only borrowed. Within minutes, the lizard *always* returns to the ninth hole with the ball in its mouth. I ask you, where else on God's green earth does somebody get the chance to buy a golf ball from a lizard?"

AN OLIGARCH'S YACHT, THE *OILIGARKI JR.*

What fitter name for the Russian oligarch Boris Samovar's personal yacht than *Oiligarki Jr.*?

The self-titled "oligarch," after all, had made his billions in the post-glasnost petroleum-export boom; legend has it that he stood first in line at the government oil monopoly's Moscow headquarters the day its holdings went on public sale in 1991. "It was so lucky for me," he recalled, "that the hundred and five persons ahead of me in line were all stricken with lead poisoning. But there is an old Russian proverb: 'Shoot first, apologize later.'"

Three facts about Boris Samovar's yacht command our attention. First, it was an exact replica of the *Livadia*, the House of Romanov's innovative floating palace launched in 1880. The turbot-shaped *Oiligarki Jr.* featured three-abreast funnels and an ovoid shape and dripped with Czarist-style luxury.

Second, it was built to cruise the man-made Lake

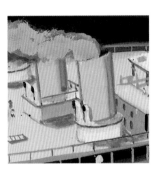

Samovar on the Crimean coast where nestled the Samovar summer palace.

Third, Lake Samovar was the first body of water in history to consist not of water but of oil—a veritable second black sea of oil, constantly topped up by tapping a nearby pipeline. A stroke of idiocy or a sentimental celebration of the liquid black gold that had made such flamboyant indulgences as the *Oiligarki Jr.* possible? Pundits differ. They bicker. Sometimes they fistfight and roll on the floor.

The final marvel of the *Oiligarki Jr.* tale was the ex-Soviet Air Force experimental vertical-takeoff-and-landing aircraft pointed skyward on the deck amidships. "It lets me get away in a hurry when something comes up," Boris Samovar explained.

Alas for the oil czar, the VTOL wasn't quick enough. The reason this tale is told in the past tense is that one balmy Sunday afternoon in 2012, on a sunset cruise when the *Oiligarki Jr.* was crowded with

This rare low-res telephoto painting catches prominent pals of owner/host Boris Samovar on a Sunday cruise on his private premium-crude-oil-filled lake. Faces have since been redacted at the pals' request in order to conceal their connection to Samovar, now in disgrace as a hooligan illegal-hole digger.

its usual complement of prominent guests, a black helicopter gunship whirred in from nowhere and landed on that deck. Boris Samovar was arrested by officers from the Crimean Ministry of Excavations for violating a little-known law—passed only hours before—against digging holes without a permit. Lake Samovar would be forthwith drained and filled in, the *Oiligarki Jr.* confiscated and converted, and Boris Samovar's oil holdings turned over to the Vladimir Putin Girls' Club, a charitable foundation. As for the mighty oligarch Boris Samovar, it has been reported that he will be digging state-ordered holes in the Siberian tundra for the foreseeable future.

GODLANDIA

J esus Christ is Lord," exclaims the Reverend Rollie Jello, the founder and sole owner of the Reverend Rollie Jello One-Hundred-Percent-Money-Back Fundamentalist Curch, "but *I'm* the CFO, CEO, and chairman of the board of this operation. Pray to Jesus!"

The reverend is seated on a golden throne overlooking his sprawling new Godlandia theme park in the New Mexico badlands. "Praise to the Almighty, keeping it warm for Jesus when He returns, God smite the heathen," he beams, sipping from the bejeweled golden goblet that will serve our Savior His favorite wine once He's settled after His trip.

A fervent apostle of creationism, Rollie Jello has known—since the day he found a flyer from a Del Rio, Texas, ministry under the wiper on his windshield—that from the instant of creation to the present spans exactly six thousand and thirty-two years, three weeks, and half a day—counting in the fact that midnight of

the seventh day, when God rested, was in a time zone eight hours ahead of New Mexico. Godlandia's layout re-creates the entire history of man on earth, showing visitors how ancient Egypt and the dinosaurs and the first balloon flight and what-have-you were all jumbled up together in those six busy centuries. "Praise Jesus," the reverend explains, "God hadn't invented the calendar yet, or the clock, so without time everything happens at once. Hallelujah, I'm a sinner who's been saved!"

Sure to be a top Godlandia attraction is the slot track that circles the park, which features a mechanical Peeping Tom caveman being shooed away from ogling a naked Eve in the Garden of Eden by a righteous mechanical Adam. Another is the life-size replica of Noah's Ark, where in case of another biblical flood ("They're the best kind," says the reverend, "because that's where holy water comes from, kiss the toes of our Savior; that's why my church operates that string of Holy Water Car Washes all through the deep

South, open on Sundays"), folks can reserve an outside cabin for their pets for one hundred dollars each, four to a cabin, cash only.

Construction will start soon on a working full-size re-creation of the Red Sea at Godlandia, parted in the middle for the convenience of strollers. But the sea will suddenly close in and give you "a real soaking, come Jesus," quips the reverend, if you try sneaking through without withdrawing funds from your bank account via any of the hundreds of ATMs posted all around Godlandia to make a personal donation to the Reverend Rollie Jello Homes Foundation Project, which is dedicated to laying the foundation for the gold-plated ranch-style palace that God and Jesus, in their weekly celestial conference call, instructed the reverend to build in the Seychelles.

But, say, aren't those oil-pumping rigs scattered all over Godlandia? What gives, Reverend? Do working oil wells belong in a religious theme park? "Why, joy abounding in Jesus our Lord," he snaps, "those oil wells symbolize the bounty of God's earth, praise our Maker, and all the stuff He packed inside it—coal, lead, zinc, and oil—like a giant piñata. And there's divine purpose: I intend to use the profits from oil extraction to finance a Reverend Rollie Jello Creationism Gas Station and Mini-Mart chain, baptisms free with every half-gallon bottle of Pepsi, rest in Jesus, hallelujah, saved again!"

Admission to Godlandia comes with a free lifetime trial membership in the One-Hundred-Percent-Money-Back Fundamentalist Church, plus $300 for shipping and handling. Sons of Ham, Israelites, and policemen are prohibited from entry by church doctrine. "But, praise Jesus, if Godlandia visitors will just cough up, hail our Savior," says the Reverend Jello, "we'll be able to pay the best constitutional lawyers in the country to ward off all the lawsuits. Hallelujah, I'm saved once more!"

FAN TANG CITY

What you see here isn't the city skyline it seems to be. Those are only life-size cardboard cutouts of New York's faraway Empire State and Chrysler buildings, towering over the otherworldly landscape of the Li River in China's Guangxi Zhuang Autonomous Region.

They aren't there for amusement or beauty. Shanghai's controversial Shang brothers, prominent developers in the go-go business climate of the post-Mao People's Republic, erected those dummy skyscrapers to create the illusion of an urban hell suddenly springing up to blight this serene and exotic backwater. A cheap, simple, and quickly successful way of lowering local land values, allowing the crafty Shangs to buy up thousands of prime parcels for next to nothing and start building a *real* urban hell: Fan Tang City. Just barely visible behind the fake Empire State Building is a sprawling Ping-Pong ball factory; similarly tucked in the shade of the ersatz Chrysler Building is the steel skeleton of what will soon be a methane gas refinery. Unseen but soon to join them: a nuclear-powered pig-iron foundry, two waste incinerators, China's second largest labor camp, and a petting zoo.

The rise of a heavy-industry city, with its uncontrolled smog and pollution, will almost certainly poison the air, the land, and the entire ecology of the Li River area and turn it into slag heaps and mudflats, a once pristine riverine system gurgling with odoriferous sludge. The Shangs have conceded that there are bound to be environmental costs to be borne; to that end, they recently volunteered the equivalent of one hundred dollars—cash—to establish a pet cemetery on the grounds where the soon-to-be-former petting zoo now stands.

The Shangs had already won a renown of sorts for their Perpetual Motion Ping-Pong Ball Manufactory Number One. Hailed as an epochal achievement of Chinese science when it began operating in 2003, it has never stopped—not because of some miraculous suspension of Newton's laws, as the Shangs alleged, but because scores of young orphan conscripts were forced to endlessly plod on a hidden underground treadmill that generated the electricity to power the machinery. Their boldly unorthodox enterprise earned the Shangs not censure but a state banquet, a three-hundred-piece all-electric carved-ivory mah-jongg set, and government favor in numerous future contracts. Including the manufacture of all-electric carved-ivory mah-jongg sets.

With a 322-person board of directors, every one a Shang, the complex industrial and financial combine behind the new Li River project must be ranked as one of the world's largest family-run enterprises. Attrition continues to claim several directors every year, lost to food poisonings, car crashes, drownings, defenestrations, mystery-shrouded vanishings, and more car crashes, but they are easily replaced. Experts estimate that there are at least four thousand Shang family members currently living, but they advise to check back in a year or so.

The Ping-Pong ball factory tucked behind the cardboard silhouette of the Empire State Building was ruled illegal by local land-use law, but luckily for the proprietors, all six members of the local land-use ministry were placed under arrest minutes later as antistate agitators and set to work at the factory, which was officially reclassified as a high-security prison.

This lucky break has given the offenders a front-row look at industry on the rise in the new China, as an average of two million Ping-Pong balls per day leave the prison/factory— many of them bouncing out. Indeed, so energetically do the balls bounce that all six ex-bureaucrats are assigned as collectors, chasing down the elusive little white globes all over the factory grounds and sometimes as far as the neighboring army firing range.

At this writing, five of the six have been sentenced to life imprisonment for spying on a military facility; word is that one now rules his cell block as Ping-Pong champ.

STEALTH JET— THE ULTIMATE GULFSTREAM

Buster "Moose" Hobb is the CEO of an aviation giant that was just awarded a four-billion-dollar contract from the U.S. Department of Defense to build one thousand new XXX fighters. "All our government work is profit rich," Buster blusters, "but this new XXX will break the bank. See, the XXX is so fast it lands before it takes off. So it actually never needs to be built, so that four billion in our pocket is one hundred percent profit."

So chummy is Buster with the Pentagon brass that as a surprise birthday gift they gave him a hypersonic stealth fighter as his personal jet. Painted in his wife's favorite shade of pearl white, the sleek speedster of the substratosphere is the only secret U.S. military weapon ever given to a civilian.

And with a little help from the Army Corps of Engineers, the U.S. Army, and several contractors who "owed me one," Buster designed and caused to be erected the world's only literal ivory tower a mile high above the clouds in rural Virginia. He'll have his pilot, on loan from the USAF's Thunderbirds aerobatic team, circle the homestead when the stealth fighter is returning from another round-the-world trip—though at speeds that render a friendly wave down to a thousandths-of-a-second blip.

"That stealth plane is a fuel hog!" Buster laughs. "Burns a gallon a second. Glad the Pentagon pays the bills!"

Mom and little Buster Junior, snug in their heated tropical-orange space suits on the gale-swept balcony of their mile-high tower homestead in the sky, are trying to time their millisecond-long welcome-home wave so Pop can get a milliblink of a glimpse as he whooshes in for a nearby landing in his ultrasupersonic stealth jet, private serial number NX oooo.

It's been another whirlwind world tour selling billions of dollars' worth of lethal aviation equipment and accessories to dictators, sultans, and military juntas—or whomever he's warned in so many words that a neighboring state (Pop will visit them on the next trip) might just be planning a missile, rocket, or, for all anybody knows, a nuclear air strike.

Once he's back home with his pipe and slippers and his Rottweiler, Adolf, at his feet, it'll be a few martinis and Fresca, and an evening of Xbox fun for Pop while Buster Junior sits across the room watching and learning "and keeping his bratty little mouth shut," jests Buster Senior—so doting a dad that he's dangled Buster Junior feetfirst off the balcony for one whole hour in the middle of a freezing mile-high night to cure him of airsickness—despite having to rise before dawn for another flight to a country next to a country that if it isn't wartorn when Hobb arrives, it ought to be by the time he leaves. Or their money back.

THE GENIUS OF NOT
BEING A SHARK

The giant shark you think you see in this picture is, according to its creator, the billionaire fifteen-year-old French enfant-terrible conceptual artist Brût Savagè-de Sauvagé, a clam.

"This physical world is but a veil that the mind pulls over itself to protect against the existential despair of knowing we will be buried wearing socks," pronounces Savagè, nephew of France's richest government minister, holder of the sole license to practice art in metropolitan Paris, and founder of the so-called Arrested Movement, which emerged last year and is expected to exert a powerful influence on the international art scene at least until next March.

"What I have endeavored to portray in this sculpture of many thousands of kilograms of concrete, many times life-size," he explains wearily, as if for the thousandth time, "is a clam *posing* as a shark. This is a

common self-protective ruse in the dark and secret world of the bivalve, or should be, and since I believe most passionately in the conditional, it thus is."

Collectors from the world over have flocked to the French-possession Crozet Islands, a former nature reserve in the southern Indian Ocean, to take the two-minute, one-thousand-euro bathysphere ride that is the only way of examining Savagè-de Sauvagé's masterpiece, anchored in the mud. A relative cakewalk for a Savagè-de Sauvagé work: last year, the art cognoscenti had to ride a hot-air balloon to fifteen thousand meters over Morocco to catch a glimpse of the conceptualist genius's controversial *Fluttering Flan* installation—a thousand dishes of flan, swirling in midair before cascading to earth and burying themselves in the sand, out of reach of starving desert urchins. "They do not understand great art," huffs Savagè-de Sauvagé.

PAINTBALLING ON THE RANGE

Paintball splatters can't fully replicate the bloody wholesale slaughter of bison herds that emptied the western plains a century and a half ago. But the thrill of drawing a bead on a huge, helpless beast and blasting away at him up close from a moving train lives on at Wyoming's Dadgum Ranch, a four-hundred-square-mile swath of open prairie with a railroad running through it.

Dadgum is the hobby of Miles Prower, owner of the world's largest money-laundering chain, who started out in life shooting squirrels in his backyard back in Pottstown, Pennsylvania, and, as his ambition and firepower expanded, voles and cats and rabbits and deer. Until one day he found himself standing in a field with a Kalashnikov submachine gun and a herd of Holsteins.

"It came to me right then," recalls Miles. "Call me a hopeless romantic and a nostalgic fool, but I realized in that instant that it was my mission to bring back those good old days. To revive that storied nineteenth-century sporting tradition of running a train full of armed and drunken revelers around and around through the grazing grounds, shooting to their hearts' content at those big shaggy brutes.

"Actually," Miles avers, "if you've ever had the pleasure, it's surprising how little it changes the thrill of the kill to use paint shot from a big-bore elephant gun. *Blam-blam-blam!* Got the bastard! The joy is exactly the same."

The locomotive is a genuine wood-fired 1880s Baldwin acquired from a bankrupt western museum of early transportation; coupled to it is a gaggle of authentic old-fashioned wooden coaches collected "from here and there," as Miles coyly if vaguely explains, shrugging off queries as to why that transportation museum curator has just been apprehended in his brand-new Tesla by local lawmen and taken away in handcuffs.

"You've got to have authenticity or it all falls flat," Miles Prower muses. "That's why I insisted on a genuine period locomotive, and why the booze served on the train is the same 120-proof rotgut they used to sell to the natives."

The pride of the Dadgum arsenal is another authentic antique—a Gatling gun converted to pepper the herds with paintballs instead of bullets. "Accuracy doesn't mean a thing," attests one Dadgum Gatling regular. "You just spray them like a garden hose and some of your shots will always hit."

Washing off the bison after they've been exposed to a day's worth of paintball fire is the job of Miles Prower's crew of wranglers and roustabouts—who also peel unconscious shooters off their seats and hose them down with chuckwagon coffee while they lie out there in the jimson weed amid the bison droppings, dreaming of guns and guts and glory.

"Later, if they can stand up," Miles adds, "they can come by the barbecue and have a thick, juicy bison steak. Can't tell you where they come from; let's just say I still have that Kalashnikov."

The basic human impulse to kill other creatures for the fun of it has been brilliantly channeled into recreational sport by bison paintball-shooting orgies. No animal is injured when a trainload of happy marksmen goes rolling by a bison herd on the open prairie, taking potshots at these magnificent beasts as they peacefully graze—and, at the worst, splattering their hides with exploding pellets of harmless paint. It is worth noting, and a tribute to these weekend sharpshooters, that no bison has ever been hit in the eye. "They're just too damn small," explains one veteran sniper. "Two needles in one humongous furry haystack. I don't think even Annie Oakley ever pulled that trick off."

But what of the basic human impulse to kill other humans? Psychologists and the NRA explain that this primitive lust has lurked deep down in all of us since caveman days. So against the day when man reverts to caveman—we've all seen the movies, aliens or some apocalypse throwing mankind back to the Stone Age—keeping that vital survival skill alive is crucial.

That's why the paintball army is permitted one shot per man at a living human being on every official outing. Not that living humans are exactly a dime a dozen out there in the bison habitat, but maintenance crews can be spotted within shooting range as they hose off the paint-smeared bison for the next trainload of marksmen or bag the beer cans and bourbon bottles and spent paint pellets that litter the trackside. Fair game! "It's like any other kind of hunting," enthuses one grizzled musketeer. "You get 'em unsuspecting, blast 'em when their back is turned or bending down. And unlike the placid bison, when a man gets hit, he reacts! Bull's-eye, then it's 'Ouch! Look where you're shootin', ya stupid drunken idiot!' Now, that's a kick. Makes you wish bison could talk. Bet they'd be bellowing really nasty curses and so forth and so on!"

FRACK KING, FRACKING FOR INCA GOLD

Freebooting Texas developer Mert Suckley pioneered the Texas Academy of Development, dedicated to instructing aspiring developers in the fine art of conspiring with politicians and rock stars to secure no-bid contracts to lease, sell, and/or build on land that doesn't belong to them. His reward? Seeing young folks succeed in this challenging career—and, of course, his ten percent cut of every graduate's future income for life.

Drawing on the fortune that followed, Mert has swashbuckled his way to even more bloated riches with one or another ingenious project: selling all the sand in Saudi Arabia to Saudi Arabia; advising the government of Romania on setting up a tax on chewing; licensing the Internet @ symbol and collecting .01 cents for every digital communication.

"I got on the fracking bandwagon early and was well on the way to turning most of the farmland in western Pennsylvania into the world's biggest swamp," recalls the self-confessed Pretender to the Throne of Hydraulic Fracturing. "Then I happened to see a World's Greatest Hoaxes Channel documentary on buried Inca gold just after reading all about the lost city of Machu Picchu in *Today's Armchair Looter* magazine and put two and two together. As the Incas say, or said, *'¡Ay caramba!'*"

Two and two added up, in Mert's mind, to Inca gold lying buried beneath the ruins of that sacred city high in the Andes. "I mean," he splutters, "why would anybody put a whole city way the hell up there if it wasn't to hide something underneath it? The Incas didn't have any

**Fracking for Buried
Inca Gold Dust**
Machu Picchu, Peru

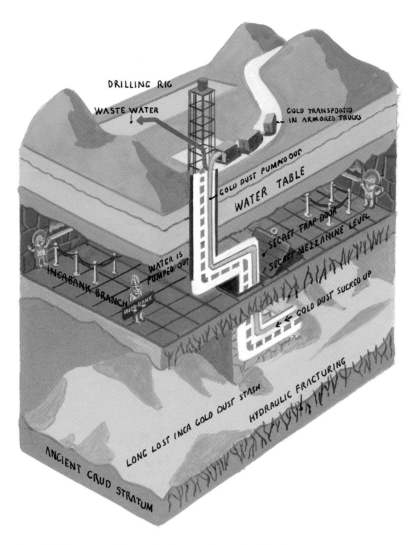

DRILLING RIG

WASTE WATER

GOLD TRANSPORTED IN ARMORED TRUCKS

GOLD DUST PUMPED OUT

WATER TABLE

SECRET TRAP DOOR

SECRET MEZZANINE LEVEL

WATER IS PUMPED OUT

INCABANK BRANCH

INCA BANK

GOLD DUST SUCKED UP

LONG LOST INCA GOLD DUST STASH

HYDRAULIC FRACTURING

ANCIENT CRUD STRATUM

oil or natural gas, but they did have gold. I call that a slam dunk of historico-geomineralogical analysis."

So his two-hundred-man crew—once the official go-ahead came through minutes after Mert's donation to the Peruvian Army Officers' Benevolent Society cleared the bank—began injecting millions of gallons of water into the ancient soil to frack not gas or oil but a billion dollars' worth of gold nuggets out of their subterranean hiding place.

Mert's plan is to melt it all down and mint gold coins and sell them via the Internet through IncaBank, already licensed by the government of Peru. "And all *that* cost me," Mert Suckley preens, "was a brand-new Jag for the girlfriend of every member of the banking commission."

This exquisitely detailed cutaway diagram reveals what goes on beneath the ancient Inca mountaintop city of Machu Picchu, utilizing the amazing new process wherein the high-tech science of hydraulic fracturing is deployed to extract the tons of raw gold dust hidden deep below the earth centuries ago by IncaBank sandhogs where the IRS (Inca Revenue Service) would never dream of looking for it.

See here how drill bits chew down through the water table, the muck and slime, the rock, the mud, the crusty shale, and the abandoned IncaBank Machu Picchu branch to finally hit literal pay dirt—the stratum of gooey nougat-like gunk where gold and dirt are all packed and jammed together in a mixed-up mess. A high-powered nonstop jet of water coupled to the drill bit then sluices the gold-flecked slurry up to the surface by a return pipe as it is stirred.

There, licensed sifters wash away all the debris to reveal tons of the glittering precious ore and then transfer it via special pans to waiting armored trucks; bonded drivers then head out in high gear for a nearby secret airstrip and a waiting plane before the authorities can figure out what's happening.

NUCLEAR
JACUZZI

Nat Mucus—yep, that same Nat Mucus, boy wonder of urban property development so famed for selling a package of old-age homes, free health clinics, and public libraries in Providence, Rhode Island, that he didn't even own to make room for the first gaming casino ever licensed to a tribe of Italian Americans—cashed out with his multimillions at age twenty-three and has been putting on the dog, and the pounds, ever since.

"Fat Nat," also famed for a weight regimen that saw him gain a pound a day for years without eating kale, most recently landed ("with a mighty thud," says live-in gal-pal Florence "Tiny" Florenza) on the tiny atoll he discovered in the outer Fiji Islands, where he decided to settle down and immediately install the southwest Pacific's first and only nuclear power plant, specifically to ensure a steady round-the-clock supply of hot water to his Olympic-size Jacuzzi.

"I paid some of the top doctors in Mexico to recommend a Jacuzzi as less taxing than diet or exercise," Nat says. "And listen, no nuclear plant in the South Pacific has ever had a power outage from toppled trees downing lines in an ice storm. Yeah, yeah, you say there's no nuclear plants in the South Pacific and no ice storms either, but let's not split hairs, you petty bastard."

Nat's typical day starts in the Jacuzzi when Tiny wakes him up; the two then splash and soak the hours away in their beachside tropical paradise until cocktail hour. "Best place to be as the sun sets is in the Jacuzzi," Nat confesses, "looking out at the boiling surf and all the dead fish ringing the shore, steam clouds enveloping the place, and no sound but that distant *whoop-whoop-whoop* from somewhere deep inside the reactor. That reminds me, I really ought to get somebody in to fix the leak."

Sitting in a Jacuzzi pretty much from sunup to sunset day after day, month after month, year after year will do weird things to your skin: pucker it beyond the wildest dreams of a prune, for example, while parching it a true fish-belly white. So what, shrugs Nat. Treating his body like a soft-boiled egg is his way of relaxing enough to enjoy the catnaps and nod-offs that punctuate his day and precede a sound night's sleep. In fact, a typical Nat day drones by in a semiconscious twilight, interrupted only when he's slapped awake enough to drink.

"Drinking is a magic shortcut to the Land of Nod," he lectures. "Particularly when the drink is a dry Gibson, hold the onion because it uses up too much of the volume of the glass that should be filled to the brim with Beefeater. Best results being what psychoneu-rologists call 'oblivion.'"

But Nat, truth be told, may not always be the most reliable chronicler of events in or, for that matter, outside the Jacuzzi. He observes the life around him in so advanced a state of stupe-faction that he barely notices the more gaudy effects on the local environment of the nuclear power plant that heats his bubbling tub of water—especially the long-term effects of frequent radiation leakage in the plumbing of his unlicensed and uninspected facility.

These go beyond the frothing corona of overheated surf that surrounds his tiny atoll and the frequent freak lightning storms. "I thought it was just my martini-blurred, heat-hazed, waterlogged vision," he admits, "until I patted my Chihuahua, Che, on the head and discovered that, sure enough, the little cutie has two of them. Do you have to give a double-headed dog two names? Another dry martini and I'll have it all figured out. Won't be able to sleep until I do."

HAPPY LANDINGS,
MOST OF THE TIME

Scant wonder that this ultradeluxe vacation retreat is seldom seen in the pages of *Architectonic Inquest* and other glossy shelter magazines. It's tucked so deep in the remotest Sierra Nevada Mountains that visitors must endure a four-hour snowmobile ride from the nearest spot of land flat enough for a helipad (that's if their copter was able to land during one of the area's frequent blizzards), plow through neck-deep snow in primeval forest gloom, then scale up an almost vertical rock wall to reach the funicular ski lift that takes them the rest of the way to the gates of Mucho Dinero.

How to get to the hacienda faster? A critical need if Skip and Irmtraud Bastinado (he owns oil-rich Abu Dhabi, she collects chocolate-covered Fabergé eggs) weren't to spend empty weekends in their four-and-a-half-square-mile hideaway hacienda. The solution came the instant Skip saw an ad in *Long-Range Catapult Lifestyle Monthly*, the international magazine of personal propulsion, for an all-weather, all-wood,

ecologically pristine transportation system capable of delivering a passenger over a distance of ten miles in sixty seconds. And reliant for its power on not a drop of fossil fuel—indeed, no fuel at all.

Six weeks later Skip was buckling Irmtraud, her luggage, and her Labradoodle, Snowball, into the spoon-shaped passenger seat of his very own ShotMaster Mark IV catapult, pointed at a bull's-eye painted on the mountainside just in front of Mucho Dinero ten miles away across the valley, a ridge, another valley, steep foothills, the eastern face of Mount Terwileger, and a flagstone terrace.

He's repeated the procedure dozens of times since. "All clear," he barks as the crew backs away from the thirty-foot-high contraption of timber and rope. Then "Fire!" An ax-wielding crew member chops the restraining rope, the catapult's powerful lever slams forward, and Bastinado's accountant, Irv, is shot from the spoon like a horse chestnut from a slingshot, tracing a perfect arc as he heads for a

A guest launched by passenger catapult across an impassable valley crash-lands only yards away from the cushioned bull's-eye target.

Vagaries of wind and weather, and the catapult's own inbuilt idiosyncrasies, make every flight an unpredictable journey. "But what can I do?" squeals owner/proprietor Skip. "That baby was brought here from a museum in Ghent and is four hundred years old. How many machines can you name that are so goddamn old and still work at all?"

Alternatives have admittedly been considered but ultimately rejected. One, a giant slingshot, boasted the advantage of simple design and even simpler operation—i.e., stretch that rubber sling back to its limit and pray—but it was never able to summon the firepower to fly a human being more than half a mile. A purely theoretical finding, however, since no human volunteer could ever be found, hired, or kidnapped for test flights.

Another potential solution was the cannon purchased from a bankrupt Bulgarian circus. The human projectile who had been shot from it hundreds of times under the big top was contracted for one more firing—not only his first outdoor shot from the cannon's mouth but also the first time he had ever been hurled violently off into the empyrean amid snow six feet deep, below-zero temperatures, and gale-force January winds—and from the edge of a rocky outcrop.

"You'd think a short guy with a bullet head, holding his arms straight to his side and wearing a helmet and goggles—you'd take him to be easy to spot out in the middle of the High Sierras in January," Skip shrugs. "But the little punk slipped away just as we'd packed the charge in the cannon. Nobody's seen him since."

direct hit on that distant bull's-eye, his screams of pleasure—so eerily like screams of horror—carrying back with bloodcurdling vividness in the thin, frigid air.

"Irv was the guinea pig, you might say," says Skip. "Once he'd proved it worked, I sent the nanny, then the au pair. Now everybody who comes for the weekend is helicoptered up to the launch site and shot over. Oh, some fainthearted people resist; a couple of New York City greenhorns bolted the minute they saw the thing. What chickens. We haven't lost anybody yet. Well, Irv did land in a snowbank once and it took three days to find him and another day to dig him out."

BURNING FOOT GOLF AND COUNTRY CLUB

He was blackballed by virtually every prestigious golf club on the North American continent for insisting once too often—once being more than enough—that the three gal-pals in his foursome play in the nude. So Lem Twert, the Vegas legend and the only man known to keep a zillion-dollar bill in his wallet, sought a measure of sweet revenge by establishing a private golfing paradise all his own far across the Atlantic on the burning sands of Africa's Sahara Desert. And blackballing the applications of every member of every decent golf club in the USA.

"Burning Foot's not like one of those hoity-toity clubs back home," Lem cackles. "Membership is a million bucks, cash, sure. But you can play wearing nothing but a bathing suit—or nothing at all. The golf carts are camels. If you hire a caddie, he's likely to be a Tuareg who'd slit your throat for a pack of Luckies, so don't ask him to wash your balls."

Sparing no expense, Lem laid down a lavish thirty-six-hole course on the Sahara sands, two hundred square miles of wavy desert dunes and hollows blanketed by vast rolls of Astroturf laid down, smoothed, and glued into one Brobdingnagian green carpet by a workforce estimated to be larger than the crews who built Egypt's pyramids. "And the beauty part of Astroturf is," smiles Lem, "you never have to water it!"

Celebrated architect Frank Gehry's distinctive touch is visible in the vast Burning Foot clubhouse, a blinding silver mirage brighter from miles away even than the African sun itself. And, seen up close, an

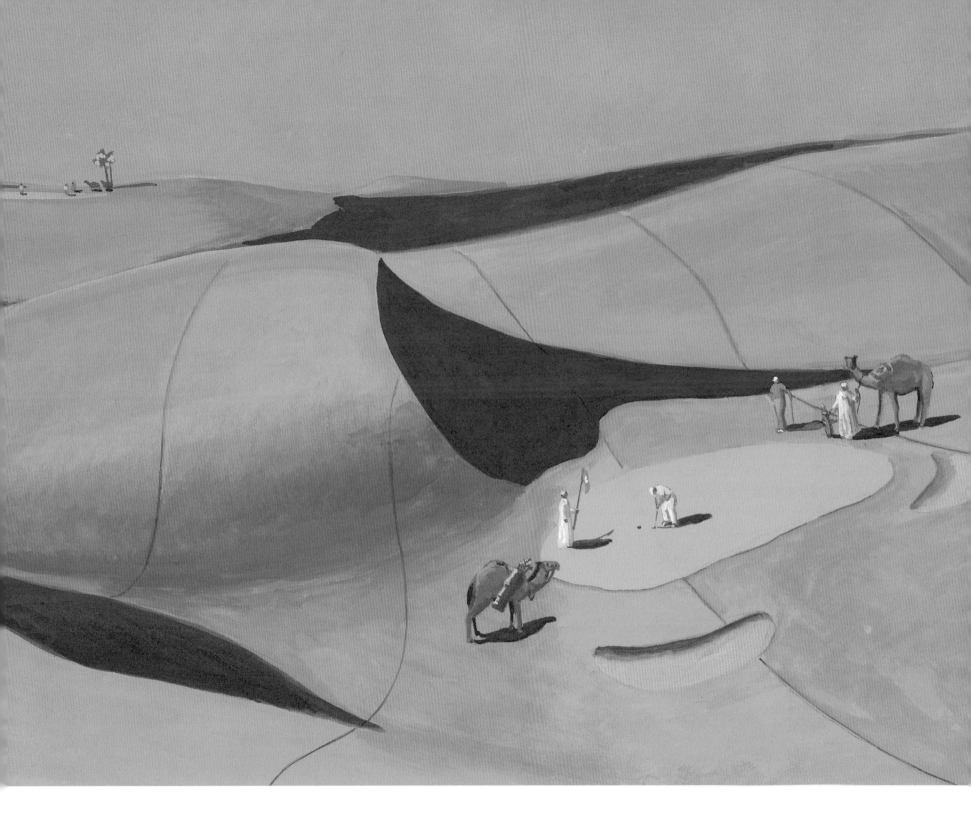

organized chaos of curved, bent, sharp, and blunt metal panels evinces that Gehry trademark of eternal impending collapse. Gehry even designed the caddie shacks that dot the links—all metal and too hot to be inhabited in daytime. "But Frank said 'no way' to air-conditioning the clubhouse or the caddie shacks," Lem shrugs. "Said it wasn't 'authentic' to have artificial cooling in the Sahara." But what counts for Lem Twert isn't comfort, it's prestige. And the prestige of Frank Gehry more than offsets a hellish lifetime of nonstop sweat.

Not that it's always beer and skittles for Burning Foot. Fierce Sahara sandstorms regularly bury the clubhouse and much of the course itself. Preservationists and climatologists inflamed by Lem's intrusion on the fragile and endangered ecosystem that is the Sahara today tend to chortle; meanwhile, Lem simply hires fleets of helicopters to zoom low over Burning Foot and blow the sand into mounds that are then removed by a dump-truck brigade and returned to the surrounding desert wastes.

"If Lawrence of Arabia played golf," muses Lem, "I bet he'd love Burning Foot. I'd give him a lifetime membership and free pro lessons. Loved that movie; in fact, I invited the Honorable Mister Omar Sharif, who was in it, to fly down and visit some weekend from his place in Egypt, but his people said no deal, not without AC. So there's ol' Lem, stuck pissing off either Frank Gehry or Omar Sharif. Sometimes I think maybe I should have stayed in Palm Springs."

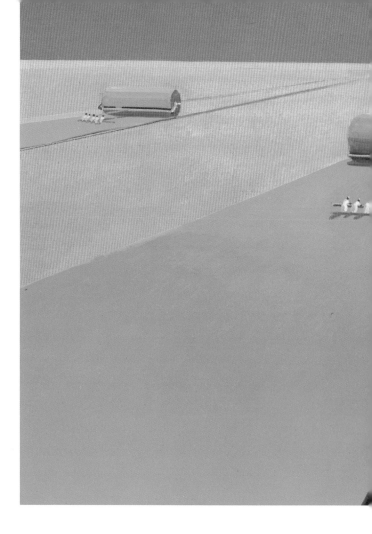

Skilled carpet layers in the southern Sahara were all booked through next year on other jobs and were jealously hoarding west-central Africa's entire supply of carpet tacks. No hard feelings: Lem Twert called in an old chit and borrowed a platoon from the French Foreign Legion base in neighboring Mali, setting the surly but burly lads to work laying down mile-long rolls of Astroturf side by side, from the oasis of Dgibidi to the oasis of Gud, until gradually, the burning desert sands lay smothered under an undulating carpet of kelly green. The Burning Foot Golf and Country Club was born.

Much hard work, of course, remained to be done. Sans carpet tacks,

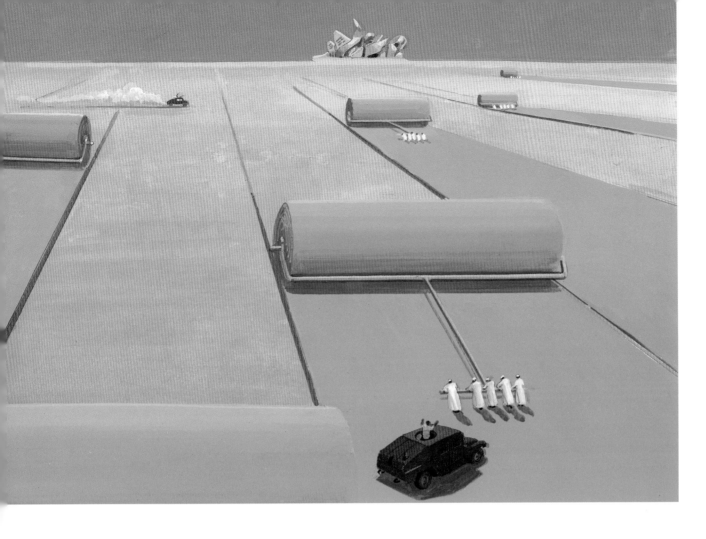

and with the loosely packed Sahara sand too deep for even fifteen-foot stakes to gain purchase, the challenge was to keep that carpet in place and slippage-free as the sandy wastes beneath shifted with the winds. Scotch tape to the rescue: binding the Astroturf strips together with this cellulose magic ensured that the vast carpet stayed in one piece.

Even at the irksome cost of sending men out nightly with jumbo-size dispensers of two-sided tape to replace what the merciless sun so often baked dry and unpeeled by day.

With even the hardiest Bedouin caddies inevitably felled by the merciless Sahara sun and the lack of charging stations rendering electric carts impractical, the ubiquitous camel was drafted to lug clubs and golfers around the course. Dromedary water storage eliminated the need for a costly underground watering system feeding multiple drinking fountains; better yet, for late-teeing golfers left stranded far from the nineteenth hole after sundown in those cold desert nights, camel dung is a guaranteed source of fuel for life-sustaining campfires.

The Gehry–designed clubhouse and the caddie shacks dotted around the Sahara have been an aesthetic triumph but less than ideal on those tedious levels of practicality and human survival. "It gets hot in there!" squeals one desert-born-and-raised caddie. "I leaned against the wall of a shack before sunset and I stuck to it like a lamb's leg to a spit." One foursome retired to the nineteenth hole for a round of drinks and never returned. Turns out, human skin shrivels under intense heat. Closing down the clubhouse that night, nobody realized that all the bacon in those chairs was the thirsty foursome.

MIND THE
FALLING
CROCODILES

Young international social actives Nicki and Vicki MacFrick took the money unearthed from an abandoned mine by her Peruvian generalissimo father and built Victoria Falls's first condominium apartment tower in the exact center of the world's highest waterfall deep in the Zambian jungle.

"That constant roar as tons of water cascade down around us is what we call 'black noise,'" explains Vicki. "Always there, always dense enough to drown out an atomic bomb blast. It *completely* drowns out the crickets at night."

"It makes me want to pee all the time," bridles studly former male ecdysiast Nicki, who since his marriage to heiress Vicki can afford to indulge his consuming dual passions of collecting cocaine samples from every nation in the world and crocodile wrangling. It's a rare hobby and a high art: "You tie the bastard down," Nicki explains, "jump on his back, throw a noose around his neck for reins—and then one of your servant boys cuts him loose and pushes him to the edge and over you go, down and down and down!

"There's only one me," Nicki shrugs, "but Africa's swarming with crocodiles." That's why he wears a parachute and the flailing croc doesn't. "And anyway," Nicki explains, "he's been around a million years and it's his country and his river. He ought to know how to handle it."

Vicki, for her part, tends to her duties as hostess at the endless come-one-come-all parties the compulsively hospitable MacFricks

seem to be perpetually staging in their lofty aerie/disco/karaoke bar with its stupendous scenic vista. The run of visitors is equally endless. "We get the most colorful people," Vicki gushes. "Exiled generals, exiled politicians, exiled tax refugees, Russian gentlemen—such nice manners, always bringing us gift crates of semiautomatics instead of boring old beluga caviar!"

No names is the only house rule.

"These people are our guests," Vicki insists. "So we don't call them war criminals or assassins or international drug cartel thugs or corrupt generals from Fourth World dictatorships on the lam. We call them family!"

The Amin Suite is on one of the condo's lower floors, where the roaring rage of the river a hundred feet below imperceptibly commingles with the rumbling thunder of the waterfall cascading down mere feet away on either side, leaving the apartment balcony perpetually drenched in spume and the occupants hoarse, even with the sliding door shut tight.

"But it's like having a second TV," burbles Vicki, "because something's always falling past the picture window. You get deck furniture, sometimes a bottle or a half-eaten piece of guava. Once in the middle of the night it was that retired Kosovar general up on twenty-seven. Some of the neighbors still whisper that it was suicide, but his arms came down separately, so how could he have got himself up on the railing to jump? He was screaming something as he flashed past the window, but unfortunately I don't speak Kosovo, so it was all Greek to me."

And there's the almost daily sight—or more like a split-second glimpse—of an adult crocodile, stubby legs flailing and long tail lashing, heading for the river with Nicki dressed in cowboy gear either riding it or just about to be detached from the saddle on its back.

"They ought to make this place a reality show," Vicki enthuses. "Although I guess it already kind of is."

INDEX

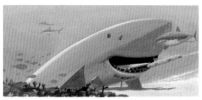

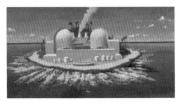

ACKNOWLEDGMENTS

Bruce McCall and David Letterman want to thank each other for making this book possible—although if the critical reception is negative and sales tank, the second edition will have replaced "thank" with "blame." But wait: our publisher reminds us that if critical reception is negative and sales tank, there will *be* no second edition. Let's therefore leave this paragraph simply as a statement of sweet goodwill and mutual esteem between the co-authors, which is actually more true than anything in the book, and move on.

Bruce and Dave equally want—no, *need*, no, *must*, no, *are morally obligated*—to acknowledge Amanda McCall's indispensable role. Amanda was handed, unasked, the thankless task of acting as what the business world would probably term Project Coordinator. This hopelessly bloodless and boring title masks the fact that we forced upon her the goddamnedest combination of liaison, interpreter, handholder, and scold, all harnessed to the bronco-busting job of simultaneously focusing Bruce and Dave's often wayward energies on the same thing at the same time, virtually every day of every week for almost three years. The book would otherwise have remained a blob of inspiration in Dave's brain and an empty space on Bruce's easel.

The reader will disregard the fact that Amanda is Bruce's daughter and worked for Dave for years; neither fact ultimately did anything but get in the way in terms of the effective completion of her appointed rounds.

In other words: she knows both of us all too well.

Thankful acknowledgment is due to Blue Rider Press and David Rosenthal for their belief in this book. Even more thanks to Sarah Hochman, dream editor/mother hen/human wailing wall and fine person. The rest of our acknowledgments here peter out in a flurry of quick thanks to Mary Barclay; Claire Vaccaro; Bruce's agent, Erin Malone, and her colleagues at William Morris Endeavor; Bruce's wife, Polly; and many of Bruce's friends for having to suffer through his unconvincing and inarticulate description of what the book was supposed to be about, up until the day it was finished.

ABOUT THE AUTHORS

Bruce McCall is a Canadian expatriate who began his career in a commercial art studio, switched to journalism and then advertising, and began writing and painting humorous subjects in the seventies, first with *National Lampoon* and ultimately for *The New Yorker*, where he has done fifty covers. McCall has published six previous books, including *Thin Ice*, a memoir about growing up Canadian. He lives in New York City.

David Letterman is an American television host.

blue
rider
press

Published by the Penguin Group
Penguin Group (USA) LLC
375 Hudson Street
New York, New York 10014

USA · Canada · UK · Ireland · Australia · New Zealand · India · South Africa · China

penguin.com
A Penguin Random House Company

ISBN 978-0-399-16368-5

Printed in the United States of America
1 3 5 7 9 10 8 6 4 2

Book design by Yve Ludwig